THE
SEVENTH
OCTAVE

THE EARLY WRITINGS OF
SAUL STACEY WILLIAMS

Published by Moore Black Press
PO Box 10545
Atlanta, GA 30310
404 752 0450
404 752 0483 fax
www.mooreblackpress.com
mooreblackpress@yahoo.com

Editor: jessica Care moore-Poole
Art Director: Pierre Bonnett
Cover & Book Layout Design: Julio Cesar Candelario
Cover Art: Marcia Jones • Waterbirth • Acrylic on canvas 24 x 30
MBP Logo: Aaquil

Library of Congress
Cataloging in Publication Data
Williams, Saul
The Seventh Octave:
the early writings of Saul Williams
I. Title
ISBN Trade 0-9658308-1-0
LC 98-065146

Published February 1998

15th printing

THE SEVENTH OCTAVE

THE EARLY WRITINGS OF SAUL STACEY WILLIAMS

MOORE BLACK PRESS

New York•Detroit•London

TABLE OF
CONTENTS

INTRODUCTION

SATURN'S RIVERS

LUNACY

THE SEVENTH OCTAVE

I

Moore Black Press

INTRODUCTION

I remember the first time I heard Saul Williams read his magic words. Like a school teacher, I prayed for the stars he wrote about so eloquently to fall into my hands, so I could place one on his forehead. What an incredible poet, the audience was full for the night. I know the masses of people are hungry, just like I was in the now famous Brooklyn Moon Cafe the summer of '95. Several seeds were planted. Maybe a meteor fell. There really isn't any scientific answer as to why poetry has resurfaced wearing new faces, shell toe Adidas, and lyrics to go. We do know the food is seasoned, matured. A well known name at the dinner table, on the mic, in movies and across the country. Here we are a few years later, in the middle of a movement without a title, unsure why poetry has become a buzz word in some circles, the way others simply survive. Eat. We represent the continuum of Black literature, Hip Hop Babies, the fluid of youth, contemporary wisdom, old spirits with new flesh.
Enter Saul Williams.
Humble in nature, his eyes seem to focus into the very souls of the listeners. Within minutes, your world is changing as Williams paints vivid pictures of parched Somali villages and red dust children. He forces you to listen to Hip Hop walking through the woods. Attacking what so many attempt to label urban, Sauls' words dance with idea that . . ."city drums mute our drums," confines languages inside zoos, and our existence as a generation.

> "I stand on the corner of the block slingin' amethyst rocks
> drinkin' 40's of Mother Earth's private nectar stock
> dodgin' cops 'cause five-0 are the 666
> and i need a fix of that purple rain
> the type of shit that drives membranes insane
> yeah, there's no repentance

oh yes, i'm in the fast lane snorting...candy yams
that free my body and soul
and send me like Shazam!

"never question who I am
God knows"
and i know God personally in fact,
he lets me call him me..."

He once told me he writes one drop at a time. It is this type of
patience that contributes to the prophetic feel of his work as
you read each line. The Seventh Octave is a poetic story that
eloquently teases with the super-natural and history while
grounding itself into the lives of everyday folks. Once you begin
to sing these words, memorize the meaning, you'll never want
the poem to end, the book to close.
Williams does what any great poet can do. Moves the
Crowd, with this sound labeled language. With an instrument
you exercise through breathing, meditation and talking shit.
Saul's young, wise voice stretches the boundaries of "religion"
without being preachy, In Untimely Meditations, he writes,

"in fact, there are no facts
fax me a fact and i'll telegram a hologram
or telephone the son of man and tell him he is done
leave a message on his answering machine
telling him there are none..."

A Khalil Gibran meets Rakim, his words swim through your sub-
conscious, an illogical wave that seems to make sense when it
hits the shore. He refuses to evaporate into the stereotypical,
and questions the evolution of a world without the need for
human life.

IV

"your evolution stopped
with the evolution of your technology
a society of automatic tellers
and money machines
nigga what?
my culture is lima beans. . ."

His voice is a weapon against hypocrisy, a celebrated new addition to the literary tradition.   A son of Larry Neal, Amiri Baraka, Ben Okri, Bob Kaufman, The Last Poets, Gil Scott Herron, Sonia Sanchez, Audre Lorde, and Ntozake Shange, Saul is easily one of the most noted and unique writers of his generation. Following in the footsteps of his contemporaries, such as, Paul Beatty, Reg E. Gaines, Asha Bandele, Tony Medina, Wood Harris, Willie Perdomo, Tish Benson, Sharrif Simmons, and inspired by many unpublished, talented others, Williams found his own extraordinary voice in a sea of writers and artists.

From Lunatics to Blind, Williams lyrical poems are stunning, full of   graphic multi-thematic word play and repetition comparable to the metaphysical rhyme schemes T.S. Eliot called the future of poetry.

I'm honored that **The Seventh Octave** is the second poetry release from **Moore Black Press**. It's an example of the power of my generation struggling to maintain our culture, critique our own voices, and celebrate our accomplishments.

"..maybe you've heard of us?"

jessica Care Moore
Publisher

V

INTRODUCTION

...."but early Sunday morning",
the preacher all but yells into the microphone.
His white beard, the glistening basin
of the waterfall flowing beneath his sermon.
He clutches his bible to his chest,
his dark fingers covering the gold cross on the cover
just enough to make me think of a four finger name ring
which transports my eyes to the two finger name ring
that is on my right hand. I got it for my birthday,
yesterday, and will sport it to school tomorrow.
The preacher repeats, "...but early Sunday morning..."
I am thinking of new ways to hold my hands
so that my new ring will always be seen.
Fingers extended, I notice the sun shining
directly on my ring (how could it miss it?)
and the beam of light reflecting off of it onto the wall.
Now the ceiling. Now begins my game.
As the preacher steps to the edge of the pulpit,
his bible still clutched to his chest,
his other hand tightly gripping the microphone,
and repeats for the third time,
...."but early Sunday morning...",
I direct the light reflecting off of my ring
directly into the preacher's mouth
and study his dancing tongue.

Saul Stacey Williams

SATURN'S RIVERS

SATURN'S RIVERS

Her newborn cyclops had my eye
but i knew i'd never claim it

i was taught not to claim
when the wind
wrote my name in the water:
waved blueness over blackness and i
at that moment i saw
that blackness would die

but not me

not we

in the deep blue abyss
we kissed on a current
and drowned eternities in loves' lost lagoons

she had hidden rooms in her womb
where i had seen screenings of the future

wrapped in swaddling clothes
and God knows i wanted to kiss it
but my lips were sealed by time

...SATURN'S RIVERS overflow
with schools of frankincense
and myrrh-maids: swimming scents of self to the soul
and sphinxes, they swim, in Saturn's rivers.
drenching the waters with ancient magic
and the secrets of the Saturn Sutra.

secrets that could name the future and
saturate the soul with stardust and samba of seasons untold
the future unfolds in Saturn's rivers
so i sailed my soul through the fore-thought of the forgotten
and waded through windows of time...

i'm certain of
SATURN'S RIVERS
and all else is fact

so baptize me in the stars
and wrap me in night-time moon blue

pupil my sight with orange balls of light
and echo my plight through the corridors of metaphor
what else are we living for
if not to create fiction and rhyme
my purpose:
to make my soul
rhyme with my...
mind

over

matter
minds create matter
minds create fiction
as a matter of fact
as if matter were fact
matter is fact
so spirit must be fiction
science-fiction
art-fiction
meta-fiction

● ● ● ● ● ● ●

RECITATION

i could recite the grass on a hill
and memorize the moon
i know the cloud forms of love by heart
and have brought tears to the eye of a storm

my memory banks
vault of autumn forests
and amazon river banks and
i've screamed them into sunsets
that echoed in earthquakes
shadows have been my spotlight
as i monologue the night
and dialogue with days
soliloquies of wind and breeze
applauded by sun rays

we put language in zoos
to observe caged thought
and tossed peanuts and p-funk at intellect
and mothafuckas think these are metaphors
i speak what i see all words and worlds
are metaphors of me

my life is authored by the moon
foot prints written in soil:
the fountain pen of martian men
novelling human toil and, yes,
the soil speaks highly of me
when earth-seeds
root me poet-tree
and we
forest forever with
recitation

● ● ● ● ● ● ●

BLIND

i was born blind and
have never wanted to see

i sense
the secrets of the stars
and share
shadows with the moon

i have learned to calculate
the brightness of black
and am afraid of nothing
but the light

i have seen nothing
yet, i bear witness
the moon is full
on every night
and every night
is every day

no one smells the same
i know how to summon
the scent of my mother
from the stars and i can smell
the stars in all souls

i am not certain of the sun
i have never seen a shadow cast

yet, i have seen shadows
cast rainbows and mountains

i am blind
i have never wanted to see

i fear nothing but light
light is the shadow of truth:
it sobers imagination and
leaves us drunk with perception

i have seen nothing and am not
convinced of the clouds
my days are
as bright as my nights

i am a star-gazer by day
and a fisherman by night
i cast my net under
the shadow of the moon
and I love the wind

i am blind
i have seen
all that there is to see

i have planted
shadows on the wind
in an attempt
to breeze blackness
over the Earth

this is a confession
you are guilty of light
repent and be reborn blind

or forever see
nothing

● ● ● ● ● ●

INDIGO ON

if i could sample the wind i would loop it
and let my life/poem flow over it's sacred beats

using Kilimanjaro as my djembe
i would drum rainbows out of the moonlight
and use them as hooks between verses

verses of little girls focused on ropes
spinning in opposite directions
looking for an opening to jump in
as the world turns double-dutch
i jump double-time over oceans and back

the water waves and i wave back:
rippling echoes of sunshine
folks get brown in the sunshine

but the lightening flashes three times
and it's time for the chorus
which includes cornbread,
candy yams and all that good stuff
that black folks and Saturn are made of

as we approach the second verse the roots of trees
are plucked for bass lines which resonate and shake the earth
devastating everything that's not in harmony with it

the second verse is a journey through the ruins
of ruined souls that valued all that was nothing
and nothing of the all knowing ever blowing wind
which is the under current of this current
blowing the funky drummer from here to eternity

but even as ruined souls backspin
the wind mills forward
and rocks steady 'til the sun hits the fader
and the chorus kicks in
then the moon yells, "go"
and we all backspin **Z u l u !**

as the moonlight shines
true blue silvery indigo light
my spirit takes flight
because the indigo moonlight is my indo

i n d i g o

indigo on
to the break o' dawn
rock rock
steady steady
'til the early morn
it's about seeing
your nature in nature
and nature in your nature

New York states of mind did not create you

not until you listen to Rakim
on a rocky mountain top
have you heard hip hop
extract the urban element that created it
and let an open wide countryside illustrate it

riding in a freight train
in the freezing rain
listening to Coltrane
my memory went insane

and i think i saw Jesus
he was playing hop scotch with Betty Carter
who was cursing him out
in a scat-like gibberish
for not saying butter fingers

and my fingers run
through grains of sand
like seeds of time

the pains of man
the frames of mind
which built these frames
which is the structure
of our urban super-structure

the trains and planes could corrupt
your train of thought
so that you forget how to walk
through the woods
which ain't good
cause if you ain't ever walked through the trees
listening to Nobody Beats the Biz
then you ain't never heard hip hop

and you don't stop
and you don't stop
and you don't...

stop letting cities define you
confine you to that which is cement and brick
we are not a hard people
our domes have been crowned
with the likes of steeples
that which is our being soars with the eagles
and the Jonathan Livingston Seagulls

yes, i got wings
you got wings
alas God chillun got wings

so lets widen the circumference of our nest
and escape this urban incubator

the wind plays the world like an instrument
blows through trees like flutes
but trees don't grow in cement
and as heart beats bring percussion
fallen trees bring repercussions

cities play upon our souls like broken drums
we drum the essence of creation from city slums
but city slums mute our drums
and our drums become hum drum
'cause city slums
have never been where our drums were from
just the place where our daughters and sons
become offbeat heartbeats
slaves to city streets

where hearts get broken
when heart beats stop
broken heartbeats become breakbeats
for niggas to rhyme on top
but they rhyme about nothing

they don't have nothing to rhyme about
'cause they've never seen the moon
your styles can't be universal
if your not intuned with the wind

● ● ● ● ● ● ● ● ● ● ● ● ● ● ● ● ●

THE WINDS' SONG

the square root of a kiss is a hum
i hum under my breath when i contemplate
the drum of your heartbeat
and my heart beats for your breath
i revel in the wind for mere glimpses

i'm tornado over you
would you look into the eye of my storm
i whirlwind through your life like breeze
and fill your lungs
as we achieve the second power of a hum

I love...

as instruments come to life through breath
the wind sends my high notes to indigo communions
with Coltranes' "Favorite Things"
...this is my body
which is given for you,
this is my blood
which is shed for you...

my love like the wind, uncaged
blows time into timeless whirlpools
transfiguring fear and all of it's subordinates
(possession, jealousy, fear)
into crumbling dried leaves

my love
is the winds slave
and, thus, is free

my love
is the wind that is shaped
as it passes though the lips of earthly vessels
becoming words of wisdom
songs of freedom
or simply hot air

my love
is the winds song:
if it is up to me, i'll never die.
if it is up to me, i'll die tomorrow
one-thousand times in an hour
and live seven minutes later

if it is up to me, the sun will never cease to shine
and the moon will never cease to glow
and i'll dance a million tomorrows
in the sun rays of the moon waves
and bathe in the yesterdays of days to come
ignoring all of my after thoughts
& preconceived notions

if it is up to me,
it is up to me.
and thus is my love:
untainted
eternal

the wind is the moons imagination wandering:
it seeps through cracks
explores the unknown
and ripples the grass
my love is my souls imagination
how do i love thee?
imagine

● ● ● ● ●

BROOKLYN

in one years time i have lived
through moments that have
seemed like years and am ever
convinced of the changing
seasons. from love to love and
confusion to confusion i have
experienced experience in tears
and smiles. but all has not been
as extreme. i am most often con-
templative, stoic, or somewhere
in between. somewhere between
self-hate and Brooklyn

i sit on a mountain of green-
leafed questions searching for
balance in the midst. i used to
rock beats over lunch room
tables, now i'm searching for
balance in the midst. i have seen
the sun set on a relationship
and gloried in the wonders of the
moon.

i have fallen in love with falling
in love only to find that gravity is
prisoner of the mind and has no
place in the soul. i now jump
and fly to love. but even clouds
are somewhat shackled to the
skies. so where is the freedom
in love?

only through the wingspan
of my dreams do i find
serenity soaring. daily lives
seem weighted down with
daily beliefs and fears.
ground level love isn't love
it's law:
restricted and concrete.

we love like oil slicked
birds pasted to oceans over
which they once soared.
Pasted to passions and
name-tagged possessions,
their wings now cruddied
and still.

i still love you all.
never drink still waters.
these waters are rippled
with the ridiculous, polluted
with the poisons of rash
passions, and waving good-
bye to each passing
moment.
And, oh, what moments
have passed.
You loving me.
me loving you.
me loving her and you.
her loving me and him
(and also him). meanwhile,
he was loving her and you.
and we all knew countless
in between.

and here i am, now, between
self-hate and Brooklyn. hating
myself for loving, changing,
and refusing to stand still when
mothafuckas seem intent on
keeping me in my place. my
place is unmapped,
perhaps undiscovered,
and surely gravity free.

loves place is in the
imagination: boundless and
unkempt. A gypsy of the soul
bearing treasures of life.

life is grand despite you all.
You all who all are me.
loving and learning.
dissecting egos. imagining
worlds and daring to live in
them. and if we were to
determine a divine reader to
observe our steps from the
heavens they would be able to
decipher the eternal meanings
of our paths. but then,
meanings are never eternal
only the sincerity of our paths.
We walk the streets and wander
the world spelling out the
secret of the stars with our
steps:
climbing mountains to dot an
"i," crossing oceans to cross a
"t", and breaking hearts...

hearts will always be broken
as log as there are intervals
between their rhythmic
beating until their beating
is a constant ohm...

ohm is the seed of the
universe as the imagination
is the seed of reality. only
through imagination do we
create as the Creator created
us, in the beginning. and
on the seventh day, there
was...now
...now the unknown
we stand, facing each other
the bouquet of our creation
between us
the blossoms nurtured in
bitter earth
the stems twisting away
from that tortured beginning
under the petals, thorns still
grow...

and this is the story of our
red rooted garden. the
place where we learned to
love and lie. and if I ever
learn to fly my wings will
be made of these very
petals

● ● ● ● ● ● ● ● ● ● ● ●

14

SUMMER SOLSTICE

we disguised ourselves as clouds
and wandered off into the night

i in blue
she in white

trailing the moon
at a distance
floating irises
pupils of the sky
gypsying the heavens
with lessons of light

it was a cloudy night
and she was with me
or at least her eyes were

peering pyramids
into my person
angled depths of death
wrought droughts of life

whatever that means

my secrets were seen
one summer solstice

if eyes can claim
the wonders of the soul

LUNACY

DAYMARES

i sat on top of the hill.
Unnoticed.
i opened my eyes at night
and stared into the darkness.
i stared until i radiated
enough energy to raise the tide,
shift the coast, and shake the land.
As i opened my eyes
those not on the hill
closed their eyes.
i radiated inner-vision.

i am
the sub-conscious
of the unconscious.
i shift the ground and make
the highest peaks possible.
Those who know me are lunatics.
The suns' fire burns them at the stakes.
Those who know me are lunatics.
Those who don't know me
don't know anything.

i am
everything
not seen, yet seen.
i am everything not scene.
i am the whisper of the universe.
My silence moves mountains.
When i close my eyes:
daymares

● ● ● ● ●

SECRETS OF SILENCE

...there's a boy on the front porch
fiddlin' with a fiddle
his life's a riddle
only the wise
can figure what he's about
his life is filled with banjos
and his uncle taught him the hambone
he pats it on his thighs when his mom cries
but the music simply brings more tears to her eyes

so she **cries** and **cries** and **cries**

she learned to hum
as her father beat her numb
when she was young
she later learned to sing
when he was hung

her vocal chords vibrated with cries to the Lord
that floated over her tear-coated tongue

now her son is on the banjo
and she sits like an angel
braiding her baby daughters hair
she humming though her past
and braiding for her future
lubricating her present
with grease and tears

her son knows the secrets of silence
he outlines them in song

painting the wind
with strokes of musical notes
that float to the clouds
and bring forth rain

only the universe
knows his pain
which is pleasure
giving silence texture
and nothingness form
he keeps his family warm
through song

Dear God,

We danced today.
Someone planted a bluefish
and it blossomed clear-water trees
and Caribbean sea leaves
and we danced circles
around the ocean
until it evaporated.
his sister prays to a salt-water god
that dwells in her mothers puddled tears
and sails popsicle ships through her fears
while her mother braids her hair
and her brother plays the banjo

they are echoes of a far off cry
children of a distant moon
holders of the secrets of silence

lunatics

● ● ● ● ●

LUNA SEE•MOON EYE

her stomach bloated with indigo silence
she birthed a nation of loud motherfuckers
that set fire to her womb as they exited
and called it
the Sun:

the father of sweat
the father of rain
out of heat comes humidity
out of fire comes water
and out of the Suns' fire-water
came the plants and trees
that call her name in the darkness

as she stares one-eyed
and raises the tide
in an attempt to kiss
the blood of her burning womb

this is my blood which is shed for
...you motherfuckers are undeserving
cyclops that she is
she still gives
even though we label her followers

luna
tics
toc
tic

the working day is over
and we rest our perceptions
under the indigo silence that she emits
as she stares into our minds eye

deciphering the universe in our dreams
and we dream of raped mothers and bastard parents
and we dream of burning crosses and Salem witches
star-crossed bitches and moon-kisses
that caress our sub-conscious like motherly hums
and play our soul-strings acoustic
until we awaken to the flames of her burning womb
engulfed in the vaginal volcanoes of velvet illusions
daylight delusions

Dear God,

    confusion. these motherfuckers are too loud and i can't
hear myself in the wind as i sing tornadoes to my children
and hum hurricanes under my breath. i'm being beckoned by
the bastards of another day. is nothing consecrated in love,
anymore? will my love/children of this generation die labeled

the working day is over and i am full
with the love/sorrows of a completed cycle i am full
with the indigo pains of a blood stained womb
as i stare one-eyed and raise the tide
in an attempt to kiss the blood
of my burning womb

this is my blood which is shed for
... you motherfuckers are undeserving

forcibly penetrating my indigo silence
in the name of the father
and the Sun

● ● ● ● ● ●

21

CHILDREN OF THE NIGHT

I

...and out of the Suns' gates come little girls in
dresses of fires, wearing pig-tails of braided smoke,
which stem from their moon-cratered scalps.
the glowing seeds of a nightly garden
that will blossom into full moons
irregardless of the Sun.
they know the night and
the seven names of the wind
through the tales of their wind-blown fathers.
Who will father these mothers of light?
And what will become of me?

children of the night,
only some will star the sky
only believers in death will die
and fathers must feather the wings of women

for the unfeathered masses dangle, ridiculous
carrying crosses to phalanx filled tombs
the future sails silence through blood rivered wombs
that ripple with riddles of cows and spoons
and births moons and earths sun-centered at noon
she buries her eggs in the soil
and plants her feet in the sky
soil seeds a circus of carrots and
clowns and minstrel shows our desires

and here i stand
court gesturing infinity
fetal-fisted for revolution
but open hands birth humility
now what is the density
of an ego-less planet?

Must my spine be aligned to sprout wings?

i'm slouched into slang steps
and kangol'd with gang reps
but my orbit rainbows Saturns rings:
mystical elliptical
presto
polaris

karmic flamed future
when Saturn's in Aries
and now i'm a fish called father
with gills type Dizzy:
blowing liquid lullabies
through the spine of time
to tranquilize a nervous systems' defeat

at the feet of forever
the children are gathered
or rather buried
in that mass grave sight of the night.
they are the seeds of light
planted in the sky.
but then nights and skies are meaningless
to their unearthly eyes.
they are our children:

playing chess on the sunburnt backs
of one-eyed turtles
checkmating a lifetimes
slow crawl to enlightenment
cashing in their crown
and glory for magic

and contradiction
the children of fiction
born of semen-filled crosses
thrust in calvary's mound
with memories of mananas millennium:
the gravity of the pendulum
the inscription of the grail
the rumors of war and famine
diseases and storms of hail

all hail the new beginning!
Behold the winters end!
bring on the puppets and dragons!
Let the ceremonies begin

for they have come to shatter time
and bring back the dead
newborn, an army of me:
bearing change on the frontlines
and shadows in the field mines
to wilderness the lights of the city.

i have seen them:

a tumultuous army
of beggars and bastards
witches and harlots
madmen and idiots
dancers and lunatics
losers and lovers
sinners and singers
students and teachers
poets and priests

orbiting the realms of the ordinary
through the ordinances of those ordained by the beast
These are our children: love laden life lanterns
casting shadows that shepherd the flocks
crying wolf when the moons full
as sirens of loves lull
the offspring of Gibralters rocks

Who will deny them when thrice crows the cock?

II

Will it be you Peter ?
decked in daymares denial
masqueraded in matter
over mind
under trial

self is the servant to serpents with wings

three is the beginning of all things
try angles when recks tangle your wings
know ye are the sum of your burdens
pile stones and unearth ancient learnings
see self as the ghost of your servings

if you're serving the father
there's no son without mother

parent bodies discover
water bodies and drown
wade me in the water
'til Atlantis is found
on the sea floor of self
i am starfish and unbound

'heard the name of that mound is Stone Mountain
under water volcanoes
erupt water fountains of youth

lest this carnal equation cancel out wind and truth
swirl me beyond sometimes
drench me waterproof
let eves drop forever
rain sunsets on my roof

as i sit on the front porch of my sanity
deciphering hambones
to van gogh this vanity

"oiled egos canvassed and framed"

to be reborn
unborn
unburied
unnamed

a reflection through a blood stained glass window
of souls gone yellow 'round the edges:
carbonated dreams
and blurred daily lives

but let family bring focus
out of swamps blossom lotus
the muddy water
blue daughters of infinity
grant we water bodied
boddhisatvas our serenity
as we rise with the tides
towards divinity

III

and she will be raised by wolves
just below the masonry dixon line
where eagles noose the misuse
of Osirus' sacred papyrus'
in their claws clench
so that the vultures
of our memories
may feast upon the remedies
of ancient laws
lynched and flock
to the tree tops

of the forethoughts we have forgotten
yes, silence will be begotten of the wind

the silver eyes of the darkness are her friends
and they sometimes plant forever in their dens
on the mountain sides of sometimes now and then
in between the rise and set of you and i

mayblu visions know the depth of liquid skies

and some ask me if she cries in the night
when it's the substance of her tears
that drench the days with light

shit, you better hope she do

'cause there are women
with fur coats and painted faces
they eat Chinese apples
that stain their teeth red
and can cackle cosmos out of chaos

at a moments...notice
the children on the train
selling chocolate
with their mothers in the background
fundraising their dreams from the dead

and the authors of autumn
correspond with catharsis
and change the leaves
of my needs orange red
i need fruit and vegetables
for only living things
can feed the span of wings

and thus she was born
to charter my flight
into the blues of night

i am the darkness that precedes the light
a pupil of the sea's reflective sight

notebook in hand
i footnote land and write

plot dot, dot, dot
and dot my " i "s as bright

and cast my lot amongst the children
and the night

● ● ● ● ● ● ● ● ● ●

THE SEVENTH OCTAVE

1987

:acid wash guess with the leather patches,
sportin' the white diadoras
with the hoodie that matches
i'm wearin' two swatches
and a small gucci pouch
(i could have worn the louis but i left it in the house).

now, my niggas, duce and wayne,
got gold plates with their names
and the skyline on it with the box link chain.
i'm wearin' my frames.
they match my gear with their tint.
and you know lagerfeld is the scent.

now, my nigga, rafael, just got his jeep out the shop
(mint green sidekick, custom made rag top).
Strictly Business is the album that we play,
"you're a customer" the pick of the day.

now, there's a nigga on the block,
never seen him before, sellin' incense and oils
my man thinks that he's the law.
but why on earth would this be on their agenda?
...as he slowly approaches the window...

...uh, uh, i've seen you before
i've been you and more
i was the one bearing the pitcher of water
i rent the large upper room
furnished with tidings of your doom or pleasure
whichever feathers decree...
yo, ralph is he talking to me?
no i'm talking to the sea/sons resurrected

i'm the solstice of the day
i bring news from the blues of the caspian
my man laughs, "he's one of them crazy mothafuckas.
turn the music back up".
...'cause i'm the E-double...

wait. but. but
i know the volume of the sea
and sound waves as i will
will you allow me to be at your service?
my man ralph is nervous. he believes his strange tongue
deceives and maybe he's been informed that he's pushing gats
(hidden in the back underneath the floormats).
"come on jack, we don't have time for your bullshit or playin'.
a salaam a somethin' or 'nother".
isn't juanita your mother?

i told you i know you
now grant me a moment

...((   ))...

at the gates of atlantis we stand
ours is the blood that flowed from the palms of his...

...hands on the plow
till earth 'til i'm now
moon cycles revisited
womb fruit of the sun
full moon of occasion
waves the wolves where they run
and we run towards the light
casting love on the wind
as is the science of the aroma
of sleeping women

lost in his eyes,
they soon reflect my friends are grinning.
but i'm a pupil of his sight. the wheels are spinning.
"yo, i'll see y'all later on tonight".

In the beginning her tears
where the long awaited rains of a parched somali village.
red-dusted children danced shadows
in the new found mounds of mascara that eclipsed her face,
reflected in the smogged glass of carlos' east street bodega.

learning to love
she had forgotten to cry. seldom hearing
the distant thunder in her lovers' ambivalent sighs.
he was not honest. she was not sure
(a great grand mother had sacrificed
the families clarity for gold in the late 1800's).

nonetheless. she had allowed him
to mispronounce her name,
which had eventually led
to her misinterpreting her own dreams,
and later doubting them.
but the night was young.

SHE
the first born daughter of water
faced the darkness and smiled
took mystery as her lover
and raised light as her child
...man that shit was wild. you should o'seen how they ran...
...she woke up in an alley with a gun in her hand...
...Tupac in lotus form Ennis' blood on his hands...

SHE
woke up on a vessel
the land behind her
the sun within her
water beneath her
mushed corn for dinner
or was it breakfast?
her stomach turned
as if a compass
she prayed east
and lay there
breathless
they threw her overboard
for dead
she swam silently
and fled
into the blue
si
la
sol
fa
mi
re
do
si
the seventh octave

i don't mean to confuse you. many of us have been taught to
sing and so we practice scales. many of us were born singing
and thus were born with scales.

mermaids, cooks, and fieldhands
sang a night song by the fire
and the ocean was the chorus
in atlantis where they sang

those thrown overboard
had overheard
the mysteries of the undertow
and understood
that down below
there would be no more chains
they surrendered breath and name
and survived
countless as rain

i am the weather
man
the clouds say
storm is coming

a white buffalo was born
already running

and if you listen very close
you'll hear a humming

beneath the surface of our purpose
there is rumor of ancient rain
dressed in cloud face minstrels the sky
the moon is my mammy
the storm holds my eye

dressed in westerlies
robed by ROBESON
OL' Man River knows my name
and the reason you were born
is the reason that i came

than she looks me in my face
& her eyes get weak
pulse rate descends
hearts rate increase

"...emcees look my in the face
and their eyes get weak
pulse rate descends,
hearts rate increase..."

its like beam me up scottie
i control your body
i'm as deadly as aids
when its time "to rock the party"

we all rock fades
Fresh faded in LaDi DaDi

"and when we rock the mic,
we rock the mic..."

but less is the feminine side
"...we rock the mic..."

ignore the feminine side

"...we rock the mic..."

i presented my feminine side with flowers

she cut the stems &
placed them gently down my throat
& these tu lips
might soon eclipse
your brightest hopes

● ● ● ● ● ● ● ● ●

SHA CLACK CLACK

i know you are but what am i?

i n f i n i t y

if i could find the spot where truth echoes
i would stand there and whisper memories of my children's
future
i would let their future dwell in my past
so that i might live a brighter now

now is the essence of my domain
but it contains all that was and will be
and i am as i was and will be
because i am and
always will be that nigga

i am that nigga

i am that timeless nigga
that swings on pendulums like vines
though mines of booby-trapped minds
that are enslaved by time
i am the life that supersedes lifetimes

i am

it was me with serpentine hair
that with a timeless stare
turned mortal fear into stone time capsules
they still exist as the walking dead
as i do: the original suffer-head
symbol of life
and matriarchy's severed head
medusa, i am

it was me the ecclesiastical one
that pointed out that nothing
was new under the sun
and through times of laughter and times of tears
saw that no time was real time
'cause all times were fear
the wise seer
Solomon, i am

it was me with tattered clothes
that made you scatter
as you shuffled past me on the street
yes, you shuffled past me on the street
as i stood there conversing with wind-blown spirits
and i fear it's your loss that you didn't stop and talk to me
i could have told you your past as i explained your present
but instead i'm the homeless schizophrenic
that you resent for being aimless
the intuned nameless,

i a m
i am that nigga
i am that nigga
i am that nigga

i am a negro

negro form necro,
meaning death
i overcame it

so they named me after it
and i be spittin' at death from behind
and putting "kick me" signs on its' back
because i am not the son of
sha clack clack

i am before that
i am before
i am before before
before death is eternity
after death is eternity
there is no death there is only eternity
and i be riding on the wings of eternity
like: yah! yah!

sha clack clack

i exist like spit-fire
which you call the sun
and try to map out your future with sun-dials
but tic-toc-technology can no tic-toc me

i exist somewhere between tic and toc
dodging it like double-dutch
got me living double time
i was here before your time
my heart is made of the quartz crystals
that you be makin' clocks out of
and i be resurrection' every third
like: tic-tic-tic

sha clack clack

no i won't work a nine to five
because i am setting suns and orange moons
and my existence is this:
still
yet ever moving
and i am moving beyond time
because it binds me
it can set me free and
i'll fly when the clock strikes me
like: yah! yah!

sha clack clack

but my flight does not go undisturbed
because time makes dreams defer
and all of my time fears
are turning my days into day-mares
and i live day-mares
reliving nightmares
that once haunted my past

sha clack clack

time is beatin' my ass
and i be havin' dreams
of chocolate covered watermelons
filled with fried chicken like pinatas

with little pickaninny sons and daughters
standing up under them with
big sticks and aluminum foil,
hittin' them,
trying to catch pieces
of fallen fried chicken wings.
and aunt jemima and uncle ben
are standing in the corners
with rifles pointed at all of the heads
of the little children.

"don't shoot the children", i shout.
"don't shoot the children!"
But it's too late.
they've already been infected by time.
but this shit is before my time...
(i need more time! i need less time!)
...but it's too late.

they start shooting at the children
and killing them:
one by one
two by two
three by three
four by four
five by five
Six by six
but my spirit is growing
seven by seven
faster than the speed of light
'cause light only penetrates the darkness
that's already there
and i am already there
i'm here at the end of the road
which is the beginning
of the road beyond time
but where my niggas at?
oh no
don't tell me
my niggas are lost in time
my niggas are lost in time

my niggas are dying before their time
my niggas are dying because of time

• • • • • • • • • • • • • • • • • •

AMETHYST ROCKS

"what i got
come and get some
(get on up)
hustler of culture"

i stand on the corner of the block slingin' amethyst rocks
drinkin' 40's of Mother Earth's private nectar stock

dodgin' cops
'cause five-0 are the 666
and i need a fix of that purple rain
the type of shit that drives membranes insane

oh yes, i'm in the fast lane
snorting...candy yams
that free my body and soul
and send me like Shazam!

" never question
who i am
god knows "

and i know god personally
in fact, he lets me call him me

i be one with rain and stars and things
with dancing feet and watermelon wings
i bring the sunshine and the moon
and the wind blows my tune
...meanwhile
i spoon powdered drum beats into plastic bags
sellin' kilos of kente scag

takin' drags off of collards and cornbread
free-basing through saxophones and flutes like mad

the high notes make me space float
i be exhalin' in rings that circle Saturn
leavin' stains in my veins in astrological patterns

yeah, i'm sirius B
Dogon' niggas plotted shit, lovely
but the Feds are also plottin' me
they're tryin' to imprison my astrology
to put my stars behind bars
my stars in stripes
using blood splattered banners
as nationalist kites
but i control the wind
that's why they call it the hawk
i am horus
son of isis
son of osiris
worshiped as jesus
resurrected like lazarus
but you can call me lazzie
lazy
yeah, i'm lazy
cause i'd rather sit and build
than work and plow a field
worshipping a daily yield of cash green crops

your evolution stopped
with the evolution of your technology
a society of automatic tellers
and money machines
nigga what?

my culture is lima beans
and tambourines
dreams manifest
dreams real
not consistent with rational
I dance fɔ· nɔ ·eaзɔn
for reason you can't dance
caught in the inactiveness of intellectualized circumstance
you can't learn my steps until you unlearn my thoughts
spirit soul can't be store bought

fuck thought
it leads to naught
simply stated it leads to you
tryin' to figure me out

your intellect is disfiguring soul
your beings not whole
check your flag pole:
stars and stripes
your astrology is imprisoned
by your concept of white

of self

what's your plan for spiritual health?
calling reality unreal
your line of thought is tangled
the star spangled got your soul mangled
your beings angled
forbidding you to be real and feel
you can't find truth with an ax or a drill
in a white house on a hill
or in factories or plants made of steel

stealing me
was the smartest thing you ever did
too bad you don't teach the truth to your kids
my influence on you is the reflection you see
when you look into your minstrel mirror
and talk about your culture

your existence is that of a schizophrenic vulture
who thinks he has enough life in him
to prey on the dead
not knowing
that the dead ain't dead
and that he ain't got enough spirituality
to know how to pray
yeah, there's no repentance

your bound to live
an infinite consecutive executive life sentence
so while you're busy serving your time
i'll be in sync with the moon
while you run from the sun
life of the womb
reflected by guns
worshipper of moons
i am the sun
and i am public enemy number one
one one one
one one one
that's seven
and i'll be out on the block

hustlin' culture
slingin' amethyst rocks

● ● ● ● ● ● ● ● ● ● ●

44

SEVEN MOUNTAINS

time is money
money is time

so i keep seven o'clock in the bank
and gain interest on the hour of God

i'm saving to buy my freedom
God grant me wings
i'm too fly not to fly

eye sore
to look at humans
without wings

so, i soar
and find tickle in the feathers
of my wings

flying hysterically
over land
numerically i am

seven mountains higher
than the valley of death
seven dimensions deeper
than dimensions of breath

● ● ● ● ● ● ● ● ● ● ● ●

UNTIMELY MEDITATIONS

the fiery sun of my passions
evaporates the love lakes of my soul
clouds my thoughts
and rains you into existence

as i take flight on bolts of lightening
claiming chaos as my concubine
and you as my me
eye of the storm
you of the sea
we of the moon
land of the free
what have i done to deserve this?
am i happy?

happiness is a mediocre standard for a
middle class existence
i see though smiles and smell truth in the
distance
beyond one dimensional smiles and
laughter
lies the hereafter: where tears echo
laughter
(you would have to do math to...)
divide a smile by a tear
times fear

equals mere truth
that simply dwells in the air
but if thats the case all i have to do is
breathe
and all else will follow

that's why drums are hollow

...and i like drums
...drums are good...but i can't think
straight

i lack the attention span to meditate
my attention spans galaxies
here and now are immense
seconds are secular
moments are mine
self is illusion
music's divine:

noosed by the strings of Jimi's guitar
i swing: purple hazed pendulum
hypnotizing the part of i that never dies

look into my:

eyes are the mirror of the
soul is fried chicken, collards, and
cornbread is corn meal, flour, sour
cream, eggs and
oil is the stolen blood of the earth
used to make cars run and kill the fish

who me?

i play scales
the scales of dead fish of oil slicked seas
my sister blows wind through the
 hollows of fallen trees
and we are the echoes of eternity
echoes of eternity
echoes of eternity

47

maybe you've heard of us
we do rebirths, revolts
and resurrections

we threw basement parties in pyramids
(i left my tag on the wall)
the beats would echo off of the stone
and solidify into the form of light bulbs
destined to light up the heads of
future generations
they recently lit up in the form of

BA BOOM BOOM OHMMM...

maybe you've heard of us

if not,
then you must be trying to
hear us

and in such cases we can't be heard
we remain in the darkness, unseen
in the center of unpeeled bananas,
we exist
uncolored by perceptions
clothed to the naked eye
five senses cannot sense

the fact of our existence
and that's the only fact
in fact, there are no facts
fax me a fact and
i'll telegram a hologram
or telephone the son of man
and tell him he is done

leave a message on his answering
machine
telling him there are none

God and i are one
times moon
times stars
times sun
the factor is me

you remember me

i slung amythest rocks on Saturn blocks
'til i got caught up by earthling cops

they wanted me for their army
or whatever

picture me: i swirl like the wind
tempting tomorrow to be today
tip-toeing the fine line between
 everything and everything else
i am simply Saturn swirling sevens
through sooth
the sole living heir of air
and i (inhale) and (exhale)
and all else follows
reverberating the space inside of drum
hollows
packaged in bottles
shipped to tomorrow
and sold to the highest nigga

i swing from the tallest tree
lynched by the lowest branches of me
praying that my physical will set me free

'cause i'm afraid that all else is vanity
mere language is profanity

i'd rather hum or

have my soul tattooed to my tongue

and let the scriptures be sung in
gibberish
'cause words be simple fish
in my soulquarium
and intellect can't swim

so i stop combing my mind
so my thoughts could lock

i'm tired of trying to understand
perceptions are mangled, matted, and
knotted anyway
life is more than what meets the eye
and i
so elevate eye to the third
but even that shit seems absurd
when your thoughts leave you third
eye-solated
no man is an island
but i often feel alone
so i find peace through
ohmmm...

● ● ● ● ● ●

HM

Through meditation
i program my heart to
beat break beats
and hum bass lines on
exhalation
ba boom
b o o m
ohmmm...

i burn seven day
candles
that melt into twelve
inch circles
on my mantle
and spin funk like myrrh
ba boom
b o o m
ohmmm...

and i can fade worlds
in and out
with my mixing patterns
letting the earth spin
while i blend in Saturn

niggas be like spinnin'
windmills
braidin' hair
lockin' poppin'
as the sonic force
of the soul
keeps the planets rockin'

the beat don't stop when
soul-less matter flows
into the cosmos
tryin' to be stars

the beat don't stop when
earth sends out satellites
to spy on Saturnites
and control Mars

'cause niggas got
a peace treaty
with Martians
and we be
keepin' them
up to date
through sacred gibberish
like sho-nuff and it's on

the beat goes on
the beat goes on
the beat goes
ohmmm...
ba boom
b o o m
ohmmm...

and i roam
through the streets
of downtown Venus
tryin' to auction off
monuments of Osirus'
severed penis
but they don't want
no penis
in Venus
for androgynous cosmology
sets their spirits free

and they
neither me
nor women be
but they be down
with a billion niggas
who have yet to see
that interplanetary truth
is androgenous

and they be
sendin' us shout outs
through shootin' stars
and niggas be
like what's up
and talkin' Mars

because
we are solar
and regardless
of how far we roam
from home
the earth remains
our center through
ohmmm...

ba boom
boom ohm...

i am no earthling
i drink moonshine
on Mars
and mistake meteors
for stars
'cause i can't hold
my liquor

but i can hold
my breath
and ascend like wind
to the black hole
and play galaxophones
on the fire escapes
of your soul

blowing tunes
through lunar wombs
impregnating stars
giving birth to suns
that darken the skins
that skin our drums

and we be
beatin' infinity
over sacred hums
spinnin' funk like myrrh
until Jesus comes

and Jesus comes
every time we drum
and the moon drips blood
and eclipses the sun

and out of darkness comes the

BA BOOM BOOM

and out of darkness comes the

BA BOOM BOOM

and out of darkness comes the

BA BOOM BOOM

o h m m m . . . . .

● ● ● ● ● ● ● ● ● ● ● ● ● ● ● ● ●

Saul Stacey Williams

A young, provocative and gifted poetic voice, Saul
Williams, was raised in Newburgh, New York. He received his
B.A. in acting and philosophy from Morehouse College in
Atlanta, Georgia and his Masters in Acting from NYU's Tisch
School of the Arts. He is the star and co-writer of the film "Slam",
portraying a poet who uses his verbal gift to get out of prison,
that won the grand jury prize at the Sundance Film Festival in
1998. Scheduled for an October feature film release.

Williams exploded on New York's poetry scene just a few
years ago, and now becomes a welcome addition to the literary
world. Saul's incredible imagery and mesmerizing use of
language brings together the spiritual world with everyday life.
An impeccable wordsmith and modern day griot, Saul is one of
this generations finest writers. Displaying the finesse and
technique of a skilled emcee connecting rhymes on stage, he is
a wonderful example of how poetry is breathing through many
of his contemporaries of poetry today. Creating language and
movement through new ideas and thinkers.
His poems are healing, beautiful renditions that resonate off the
page and any readers imagination. Williams fearlessly questions
technology without humanity, poetry without it's roots. Sauls
work has appeared in the New York Times, in defense of
Mumia, African voices, Red Clay Magazine and several other
literary publications.

Enjoy the journey, the rebirth, the Seventh Octave.

Marcia Jones is a New York based visual artist who attended
Clark Atlanta University in Atlanta. When she's not painting,
she's busy raising their beautiful daughter, Saturn.

-JCM-

Moore Black Press
-Representing the literary future-

Other books by
Moore Black Press

The Words Don't Fit In My Mouth
A book of poetry by
Jessica Care Moore
Published August 1997

1998 releases

• The Seventh Octave
A book of poetry by
Saul Williams

• Fubraction
A book of poetry by
Sharrif Simmons

1999 releases

The poetry of MC's
an anthology of
lyrics,poetry,essays
and literary madness.

• An Anthology of
new woman poets
(working title)

• SugarDoe
A novel by T. Tara Turk

This is only the beginning.